COMPREHENSION
DETECTIVE

Grades 3-5

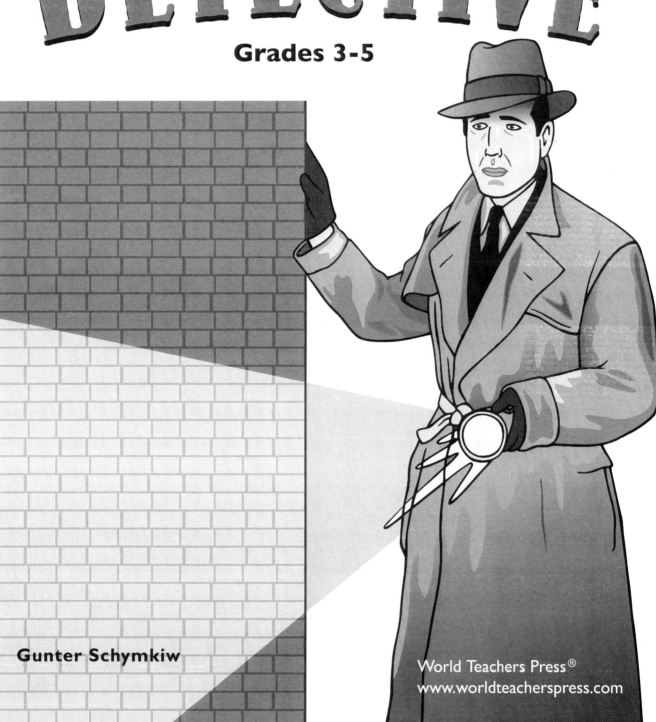

Gunter Schymkiw

World Teachers Press®
www.worldteacherspress.com

Order Number 2-5221
ISBN 978-1-58324-178-3

L M N O P 19 18 17 16 15

395 Main Street
Rowley, MA 01969
www.didax.com

Foreword

The Comprehension Detective series offers students opportunities to think critically, logically, and creatively to solve problems.

Each problem-solving activity is in the context of a short mystery story which students should find both challenging and stimulating, as they are put in the situation of being a detective whose task is to solve a crime.

To do this, they must gather information by responding accurately to a series of text-related questions. From the information collected, they are required to make connections and draw logical conclusions to solve each short mystery.

While the main focus of the activities is thinking logically or creatively within the literary framework, various other learning areas are covered.

Students will respond with enthusiasm to the challenges presented to them in this book.

Also available in this series:

Comprehension Detective, Grades 6 to 8

Contents

Teacher's Notes

The mystery story genre is a favorite of fiction. The Comprehension Detective series provides students with a broad range of comprehension and critical thinking activities.

The major questioning types and styles of thinking addressed by this book include:

Literal	–	Recognizing related information in text.
Evaluative	–	Making judgments using own opinions or related to defined standards.
Analysis	–	Thinking critically. Examining the components of a text or scenario.
		Making inferences.
		Drawing conclusions.
Synthesis	–	Reorganizing information to examine alternative possibilities.

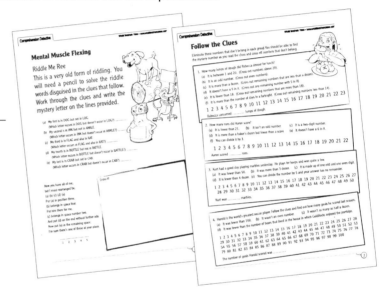

Pages 7 – 11 provide a fun introduction to the style of activities in the book. Each activity consists of one page.

Students are required to think logically, through following explicit instructions to solve a selection of puzzles.

The remainder of the book consists of two-page activities. The main focus of the activities are for the students to think critically, logically, and creatively to solve problems.

A stimulating story challenges students to take on a role of a "detective" whose job it is to solve a "mystery."

In order to achieve a solution, students must gather information by responding accurately to a series of text-related questions.

Literal questioning plays a large part in this process. Like good detectives, students must then use evaluative and inferential techniques to analyze this information. From this analysis they are asked to offer a plausible solution to the mystery.

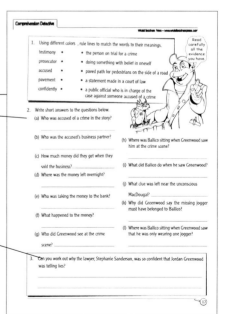

Skills Overview

Students who successfully complete the activities in this book will have demonstrated the following skills:

Skill	Mental Muscle Flexing Page 7	Follow the Clues Page 8	Pilfered Purse Page 9-10	Eliminating Suspects Page 11	Grubby Gregory Pages 12-13	The Fast-Footed Felon Pages 14-15	Colin the Coin Con Man Pages 16-17	Fresh Fruit-O for Sale-O! Pages 18-19	The Big Strike Pages 20-21	The Man in Red Sneakers Pages 22-23
locate information in a text		✦	✦	✦	✦	✦	✦	✦	✦	✦
answer literal questions			✦		✦	✦	✦	✦	✦	✦
use critical thinking to analyze text and solve problems			✦	✦	✦	✦	✦	✦	✦	✦
synthesize information to formulate solutions	✦	✦				✦				
evaluate information and make logical judgments based on this evaluation			✦		✦	✦		✦	✦	✦
apply knowledge to assist in problem solving		✦		✦			✦			
use technical knowledge to assist in problem solving							✦	✦		
complete well-known proverbs										
locate information using a variety of reference tools			✦				✦	✦		
draw inferences to make generalizations about a text					✦					
use a dictionary to find the meaning of unknown words								✦	✦	
draw on a personal experience to make observations										✦
manipulate sounds in words to solve puzzles								✦		
sequence events logically in a text			✦							
apply understandings at a creative interpersonal level					✦					
match like things from different categories				✦		✦				
make illustrations	✦									
reflect personally on a text										
link words to their synonyms										✦
examine ideas critically from different perspectives			✦		✦					
make associations			✦	✦					✦	
identify things by attribute				✦		✦				
write a brief exposition to support a particular point of view			✦		✦	✦	✦	✦	✦	✦

Skills Overview

Students who successfully complete the activities in this book will have demonstrated the following skills:

Skill	The Guilty Gambler Pages 24–25	Snow Job Pages 26–27	The Big Burger Bungle Pages 28–28	Farmer McSwine Pages 30–31	Good Morning, Sunshine Pages 32–33	The Botched Birthday Burgle Pages 34–35	The Great Diamond Grab Pages 36–37	The Breakfast Break-in Pages 38–39	Who Got the Job? Pages 40–41	Save the Panther 42–43
locate information in a text	✦	✦	✦	✦	✦	✦	✦	✦	✦	✦
answer literal questions	✦	✦	✦	✦	✦	✦	✦	✦	✦	✦
use critical thinking to analyze text and solve problems	✦	✦	✦	✦	✦	✦	✦	✦	✦	✦
synthesize information to formulate solutions	✦				✦		✦			
evaluate information and make logical judgments based on this evaluation	✦	✦	✦	✦	✦	✦	✦	✦	✦	✦
apply knowledge to assist in problem solving					✦				✦	
use technical knowledge to assist in problem solving				✦	✦		✦		✦	✦
complete well-known proverbs				✦						
locate information using a variety of reference tools		✦			✦				✦	✦
draw inferences to make generalizations about a text										
use a dictionary to find the meaning of unknown words										
draw on a personal experience to make observations				✦	✦					
manipulate sounds in words to solve puzzles			✦							
sequence events logically in a text		✦	✦				✦	✦		
apply understandings at a creative interpersonal level						✦				
match like things from different categories										
make illustrations										
reflect personally on a text						✦				
link words to their synonyms	✦						✦			
examine ideas critically from different perspectives					✦	✦				
make associations						✦				
identify things by attribute						✦			✦	
write a brief exposition to support a particular point of view	✦	✦	✦	✦	✦	✦	✦	✦		✦

Mental Muscle Flexing

Riddle Me Ree

This is a very old form of riddling. You will need a pencil to solve the riddle words disguised in the clues that follow. Work through the clues and write the mystery letter on the lines provided.

(a) My first is in DOG but not in LOG.
      (Which letter occurs in DOG but doesn't occur in LOG?) _____

(b) My second is in INK but not in ANKLE.
      (Which letter occurs in INK but doesn't occur in ANKLE?) _____

(c) My third is in FLAG and also in RAT.
      (Which letter occurs in FLAG and also in RAT?) _____

(d) My fourth is in BOTTLE but not in BATTLE.
      (Which letter occurs in BOTTLE but doesn't occur in BATTLE?) _____

(e) My last is in CRAB but not in CAB.
      (Which letter occurs in CRAB but doesn't occur in CAB?) _____

Now you have all of me,
but I must rearranged be.
(a) (b) (c) (d) (e)
Put (a) in position three.
(b) belongs in space four.
Put him there for me.
(c) belongs in space number two.
And put (d) on the end without further ado.
Now put (e) in the remaining space.
I'm sure there's one of these at your place.

___ ___ ___ ___ ___
  1   2   3   4   5

Draw it!

Follow the Clues

Eliminate those numbers that don't belong in each group. You should be able to find the mystery number as you read the clues and cross off numbers that don't belong.

1. How many muffins did Rebecca devour for lunch?

   (a) It is between 1 and 20. (Cross out numbers above 20).

   (b) It is an odd number. (Cross out even numbers).

   (c) It is more than a dozen. (Cross out remaining numbers that are less than a dozen).

   (d) It doesn't have a 5 in it. (Cross out any remaining number with 5 in it).

   (e) It is fewer than 18. (Cross out remaining numbers that are more than 18).

   (f) It is more than the number of days in two weeks. (Cross out remaining numbers less than 14).

   1 2 3 4 5 6 7 8 9 10 11 12 13 14 15 16 17 18 19 20 21 22 23

   Rebecca consumed _____ muffins.

2. How many runs did Aaron score?

   (a) It is fewer than 21.   (b) It isn't an odd number.

   (d) It is more than a baker's dozen but fewer than a score.   (c) It is a two-digit number.

   (f) You can divide it by 3.   (e) It doesn't have a 6 in it.

   1 2 3 4 5 6 7 8 9 10 11 12 13 14 15 16 17 18 19 20 21 22

   Aaron scored _____ runs.

3. Kurt had a good day playing marbles yesterday. He plays for keeps and won quite a few.

   (a) It was fewer than 50.   (b) It was more than 3 dozen.   (c) It is made up of one odd and one even digit.

   (d) It is fewer than 4 dozen.   (e) You can divide the number by 5 and your answer has no remainder.

   1 2 3 4 5 6 7 8 9 10 11 12 13 14 15 16 17 18 19 20 21 22 23 24 25 26 27
   28 29 30 31 32 33 34 35 36 37 38 39 40 41 42 43 44 45 46 47 48 49 50

   Kurt won _____ marbles.

4. Harold is the world's greatest soccer player. Follow the clues and find out how many goals he scored last season.

   (a) It was fewer than 100.   (b) It wasn't an even number.   (c) It wasn't as many as half a dozen.

   (d) It was fewer than the number of bears that lived in the house in which Goldilocks enjoyed the porridge.

   1 2 3 4 5 6 7 8 9 10 11 12 13 14 15 16 17 18 19 20 21 22 23 24 25 26 27 28
   29 30 31 32 33 34 35 36 37 38 39 40 41 42 43 44 45 46 47 48 49 50 51 52 53 54 55
   56 57 58 59 60 61 62 63 64 65 66 67 68 69 70 71 72 73 74 75 76 77 78 79 80 81 82
   83 84 85 86 87 88 89 90 91 92 93 94 95 96 97 98 99 100

   The number of goals Harold scored was _____.

The Case of the Pilfered Purse

As I knocked on the door of the neat little apartment, I was met by the fierce barking of a dog. "Stop, Butch! No!" came the rebuke of its owner.

The door opened and I was greeted by a tired, drawn looking young lady by the name of Sarah Sontner. "Ah, hello, Miss Sontner," I said, "I'm Detective Lucy Avila. I'm here concerning your stolen purse."

"Oh, thank goodness you're here," sighed Miss Sontner. Butch, a poodle-Maltese cross, sat growling, not taking his eyes from me. "Quiet, Butch! Oh, I'm sorry. He always barks and growls at strangers. Now about my purse. I really hope you can find it. Not only did it contain $5,000 in cash, but it had my credit cards, ID, everything…all missing."

She burst into tears. All I could do was comfort her and wait till she regained her composure. Butch maintained his glare and began barking on several occasions.

"Okay, Miss Sontner, can you tell me what happened?" I asked.

"Well," she replied, "I'd just been downtown with my boyfriend, Adrian. I'm new to New York…only been here a day.

"Adrian just flew in for a short visit from L.A. He's just popped out for a couple of hours to attend to some business."

As she spoke there was a knock at the door. Once again Butch began his frenzied barking.

"It's only me, Elmer, the mailman," came the voice from outside. "Got a package for you… err, Miss Sontner…is that right?"

Miss Sontner went to the door, restraining Butch and took the package. All the while Butch barked and growled ferociously.

"Say, Lady…better do something about that dog of yours before the neighbors start complaining," said the mailman.

"Oh, he'll be a lot better after a week or so when he gets to know you. He's just afraid of strangers. Once he trusts you, you won't even know he's here. Thank you."

"Miss Sontner, please, could we get back to what happened?" I asked.

"Well as I was saying, I'd just been downtown. Adrian left to attend to some business.

"I was tired so I lay down to have a little catnap. I only dozed lightly for about ten minutes, but when I woke up my purse was gone. Someone must, somehow, have opened the door and taken it while I was dozing. But, I don't understand how whoever it was got out of here without being torn limb from limb by Butch. Oh, what am I going to do?"

As she spoke there was the sound of a key opening the apartment door. Adrian entered.

Butch, as quietly as a mouse, ran to him wagging his tail and panting happily.

"Hey there, boy. Good dog!" said Adrian. "Well anything new happen while I was out? Say… Sarah…you okay?"

"No she's not, Mr. Corney. While you were out someone helped themselves to her purse. But then I don't need to tell you, do I? I think you know a fair bit about it already. I'd like to ask you a few questions down at the station."

1. Write short answers below:

    (a) List the five characters in the story. _____

    (b) What had been stolen? _____

    (c) What breed of dog was Butch? _____

    (d) How did Butch react to strangers? _____

    (e) Which three things are we told were missing from Miss Sontner's purse? _____

    _____

    (f) How long had Miss Sontner been in New York? _____

    (g) Who had come to visit her? _____

    (h) Who else came to the apartment while Detective Avila was interviewing Miss Sontner? _____

    _____

    (i) What was Miss Sontner doing when the theft took place? _____

    (j) What did Miss Sontner say she couldn't understand? _____

    (k) How did Butch behave when Adrian Corney entered the apartment? _____

2. Because you are a clever detective you probably know why detective Avila is suspicious of Adrian Corney. Tell us why in a few sentences.

    _____

    _____

    _____

    _____

    _____

3. Write a dictionary meaning of THESAURUS. _____

    _____

4. Use a thesaurus (book or online) to find three synonyms for each of these words:

    (a) rebuke _____

    (b) wary _____

    (c) purse _____

    (d) conclusion _____

Eliminating Suspects

1. Can you spot the President of the United States in the year 3000?

   This class photo was taken when he was at school in 2960.
   Read the clues and circle the ones that don't belong.
   The one remaining is the correct answer.

   (a) He had an even number of hairs on his head.

   (b) His shirt did not have a pocket.

   (c) He was not wearing glasses.

   (d) He wore a tie.

   (e) His shirt had a pattern of triangles on it.

   (f) His tie was black.

   The President is _____

   (g) The President is the only one wearing a yellow shirt.
   Color his shirt and then color the shirts of the remaining
   boys in his class blue.

2. Can you pick the $11 note from the year 3000?
   Read the clues and circle the ones that don't
   belong. The remaining note is the correct one.

   (a) It has four sides.

   (b) It has "United States" written on it.

   (c) The $11 appears in each corner.

   (d) It has a person on it.

   (e) The person is not wearing a hat.

   (f) The person is older than 20 years.

   The correct note is _____

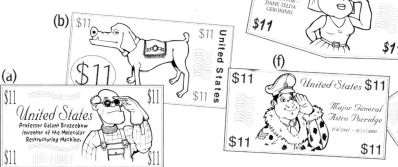

Grubby Gregory

What a shame Gregory was such a messy boy. Discarded clothing and socks were left all over the floor. The house was littered with half-full drinking glasses.

Toys were left outside in the yard when he had finished playing with them. Many times a favorite baseball bat, football, or other toy was ruined by overnight rain. Gregory felt it was his mother's job to take plates, bowls, spoons, and glasses to the sink. In fact, Gregory never put anything back in its place. That was Mom's job!

But it wasn't all bad news. Gregory was a pleasant, happy boy—just a bit thoughtless.

"If you weren't so messy, you'd be perfect," his mother said.

Even though she missed him, Gregory's mother was pleased when he went away to camp for a week. It meant that she could really clean her house. When Gregory returned on Friday evening, he was exhausted.

"I'm going straight to bed, Mom," he said.

"But you haven't eaten," said his mother.

"I have. We stopped at The House of Grease and I had an O'Grease Hyperburger," replied Gregory.

"Okay, brush your teeth and go to bed then," said his mother.

Gregory's mother ironed for about an hour and decided it was time for her to go to sleep as well. She took her toothbrush from the rack next to Gregory's and took the tube of toothpaste from its place under the sink. When she went to bed she was feeling quite pleased with herself. At last her house was tidy and this made her feel good.

After five minutes she got up again.

"Gregory, get out of bed and brush your teeth right now!" she called loudly in a frustrated tone.
👁

Use your detective skills just like Gregory's mother did and figure out how she knew Gregory hadn't brushed his teeth.

1. Write short answers to the questions below.

   (a) What sort of boy was Gregory? _____

   (b) What did he do with his socks when he undressed? _____

   (c) Name two things that were left out overnight and were ruined by rain.

   _____   _____

   (d) What did Gregory never do? _____

   (e) Why was his mother pleased when Gregory went to camp for a week?

   (f) How did Gregory feel after returning from camp?

   (g) What did he want to do? _____

   (h) What did his mother ask him to do before going to bed? _____

   (i) What did his mother do for about an hour? _____

   (j) Where was the toothpaste? _____

   (k) Where was Gregory's mother's toothbrush? _____

   (l) Where was Gregory's toothbrush? _____

   (m) Why did Gregory's mother feel pleased when she went to bed?

   (n) What did Gregory's mother tell him to do five minutes after she went to bed?

2. Good detectives take notice of people's habits. Gregory's mother knew her son's habits so well that she knew he hadn't brushed his teeth. How did she know this?

The Fast-footed Felon

Denver Pike was not someone any person would call a friend. Even though he was quite clever, he had not put his talent to good use. He was lazy and untrustworthy.

One thing that Denver could do well, however, was run. With so much natural talent as an athlete, he had been approached by a number of football teams to play for them. But Denver was too lazy to stand up to the hard training required of a top level player. He had another use for his great speed.

Denver snatched people's wallets, purses, or handbags. Once he had done this it was impossible for his surprised victims to catch him as he made a speedy getaway.

With the proceeds of his robberies he'd been able to buy his latest pride and joy, a shiny new motorcycle. All he had to do was register it and he'd be as free as a bird.

Denver turned the handle and pushed open the door of the motor registry office. He took a ticket and sat down to wait his turn. As he sat waiting, he noticed that the man two seats up from him had placed his keys and wallet on the seat between them.

Denver could see that the wallet was bulging with bills. His nasty little mind saw this as easy pickings. The man was in his fifties; no match for the speedy 20-year-old Denver.

Unable to resist, Denver picked up the wallet, ran to the door, turned the handle and pushed the door to open it. What had happened? The door did not budge no matter how hard he pushed.

Unfortunately for Denver, the man caught him easily. In fact, he caught Denver before he left the motor registry office. ◉

Can you use your detective skills to find out why Denver's little scheme fouled up?

1. Write short answers to these questions.

(a) Name two of Denver Pike's bad qualities.

_____

_____

(b) Name two of his good qualities.

_____

_____

(c) Why did Denver fail as a top level football player?

_____

_____

(d) What did Denver use his speed for?

_____

_____

(e) What had he bought with the proceeds of his

robberies? _____

(f) Why did he go to the registry office?

_____

_____

(g) What two things did Denver do to the door to enter the registry office?

_____

_____

(h) What did he notice on the seat near him?

_____

(i) What did Denver do to open the door when trying to make his escape?

_____

(j) Where did the man catch up with Denver?

_____

_____

2. Denver would be "as free as a bird" when he had his motorcycle registered. This expression is a SIMILE. Similes compare things from different groups that are alike. Choose words from the word bank to complete the similes.

bat   nails   daisy   mouse   hills   bee

(a) as busy as a _ _ _ _   (b) as tough as _ _ _ _ _ _

(c) as blind as a _ _ _ _   (d) as quiet as a _ _ _ _ _ _

(e) as old as the _ _ _ _ _ _   (f) as fresh as a _ _ _ _ _ _

3. Can you see where Denver fouled up? Write your answer in one or more sentences.

_____

_____

Colin, the Coin Con Man

Dion was excited. He had been saving his allowance for more than a year. Now, with over $200 in his pocket, he was going to the city to buy some coins for his collection.

"Here we are," said Dad as they stood at the entrance of Colin's Coin Shop.

The owner of the shop, Mr. Colin Ryan, welcomed them. Dad told Mr. Ryan that Dion had been saving hard and that he wanted to add to his growing coin collection.

"I think we should have something that he will like," said Mr. Ryan. "Here is our range of early American coins," he said, pointing to a tray on which the coins were displayed.

"And what are the big silver coins?" asked Dion.

"They're old American dollars. Very popular among collectors," said Mr. Ryan.

Dion looked at the coins on display but could not make up his mind.

"Look," said Mr. Ryan, "I have something special that I'm sure you'd like."

He went to his safe and pulled out a small, dull-colored coin.

"What I have here," whispered Mr. Ryan, "is a coin from Ancient Rome. It's over two thousand years old."

"Who's this on the front?" asked Dion.

"That's the famous Roman Emperor, Julius Caesar," said Mr. Ryan. "As you probably learned at school, he sailed over to England and conquered it in 55 B.C." Dion turned over the coin. On the other side was the Roman eagle and the date, 55 B.C.

"Wow, it really is over two thousand years old!" said Dion excitedly. "55 B.C.! I think I'll take this one. What do you think, Dad?"

"I'll even drop the price from $500 to $200 for you," interrupted Mr. Ryan.

"You can drop it to $2 and we still won't be buying," said Dion's dad. "Come on, son, we're leaving. I wouldn't buy anything from this crook."

Why was Dion's dad suspicious of the coin dealer? Like a good detective, you must find the answers to the important questions and draw conclusions from the evidence you gather.

1. Write short answers to these questions.

(a) What did Dion collect?

_____

(b) For how long had he been saving his money?

_____

(c) How much money did he have in his pocket?

_____

(d) Why was he going to the city with his dad?

_____

_____

(e) Who was the owner of Colin's Coin Shop?

_____

(f) Which coins did Dion look at first of all?

_____

_____

(g) What were the large silver coins?

_____

(h) Describe the coin that Mr. Ryan pulled out of the safe. _____

_____

(i) Where was the coin from?

_____

(j) Who was on the front of the coin?

_____

(k) What date was on the back of the coin?

_____

(l) What did Dion's dad say that Mr. Ryan was?

_____

2. Write the dictionary meaning of "obverse" and "reverse" sides of a coin.

obverse _____

_____

reverse _____

_____

3. What is meant by the initials:

B.C.? _____

A.D.? _____

4. How did Dion's dad know that the coin dealer was dishonest?

_____

_____

_____

_____

_____

_____

_____

Fresh Fruit-O for Sale-O!

"Officer! Stop that boy! He's been stealing from my shop for weeks. Those strawberries in his lunch box have just been taken from my shop!"

The agitated man was Mr. George from "George's Fine Fruit Shop" and he was asking the young police officer, Samantha O'Brian, to stop a local rascal by the name of Evan Gussey.

"Well, young man, what have you got to say?" asked the police officer.

"I don't know what he's talking about," said Evan.

"You young devil!" shouted Mr. George. "Those strawberries in that lunch box have just been stolen from my shop!"

"Well," said the policewoman, "there are rather a lot there. Where did you get them from, young fellow? Just tell us the truth. If they're not from Mr. George's shop you won't be in any trouble."

"On the weekend we went to my Uncle Paul's farm. It's about five hundred miles from here. He's got a big strawberry tree.

"We picked them there. Mom gave me these to eat while I was at my friend Stanley's place. That's where I'm going now."

"I think you're going to get there a bit later," said Officer O'Brian. "First of all, we'll go back to your place and have a word with your mother and father. Perhaps then we'll get the truth."

George's Fine Fruit Shop
for the freshest in town

strawberries $ 1.30
nectarines $ 5.70
mangoes $ 1.50

189 Cantaloupe Lane, Melonville

Why didn't Officer O'Brian believe Evan's story?

1. Write short answers to these questions.

(a) List the three main characters in this story.

_____

_____

_____

(b) Who claimed that a crime had been committed?

_____

(c) What did Mr George accuse Evan of doing?

_____

(d) What container were the strawberries in?

_____

(e) Where did Evan claim the strawberries came

from? _____

(f) What did he say he picked them from?

_____

2. All of the fruit and vegetables in the word bank can be bought in Mr George's fruit shop. See if you can find them in the puzzle. Use different colors to mark them. One has been done for you

plum, strawberry, pineapple, apricot, apple, orange, peach, persimmon, nectarine, pea, blackberry, avocado, banana, grapefruit, fruit

P	A	P	P	S	I	O	N	N	P	P	E
I	I	R	E	R	M	M	C	E	L	U	A
N	C	O	T	B	L	A	T	A	S	M	C
E	E	L	E	B	K	C	I	R	T	R	H
A	P	P	R	R	Y	A	N	E	A	A	W
B	A	N	A	N	O	V	A	M	P	E	B
F	E	P	A	A	C	N	N	E	P	R	R
R	T	A	E	P	A	I	D	G	L	E	Y
U	I	R	G	O	D	R	A	N	A	R	O

3. Write the dictionary meaning of "strawberry."

_____

_____

_____

4. At least part of Evan's story is a lie. Write what is wrong with it.

_____

_____

_____

The Big Strike

The workers of Mingey City were angry. They felt that they were underpaid for all the hard work they did.

Meanwhile, the city managers were well looked after and paid handsome salaries.

At last a meeting was held to decide what should be done. The council that employed them was a wealthy one and the workers felt that they were not being treated fairly.

At the meeting, it was decided that there was only one course of action they could take. They would go on strike immediately.

To make their point they would hold a big rally in the main street of the city. Each person would carry a protest sign.

The next morning they assembled for the rally.

Mr. Nutter, the schoolmaster, thought that his sign was very clever, indeed. "Man cannot live on chalk alone!" it read.

Mr. Binns, who drove the garbage truck, had "Our pay deal is nothing but rubbish!" emblazoned on his sign.

"Our council has gone to the dogs!" was written in angry writing by Mr. Houndstooth, the dog catcher.

Today's weather:
65°F and storm clouds gathering this morning.

Because you are a clever comprehension detective you will be able to figure out what the striking signwriters had written on their signs, won't you?

Make up some of your own clever signs for striking workers. Write the type of worker under the signs.

1. Write short answers to the questions below.

   (a) Why were the workers of Mingey City unhappy? _____

   (b) Why weren't the city managers unhappy? _____

   (c) What did the workers decide to do? _____

   (d) What is meant by "going on strike"? _____

   (e) What did the workers plan to hold in the main street? _____

   (f) What would each person carry? _____

   (g) What was written on Mr. Nutter's sign? _____

   (h) What was Mr. Houndstooth's job? _____

   (i) What job does a signwriter do? _____

2. Many last names have their origins in occupations; for example, Baker, Carpenter, Carter, etc. In Mingey City, Sean Lamb is a shearer, Tom Mix works at the cement works and Ivor Pane fixes broken windows. Make up some more people's names to match the work they do.

   _____

   _____

   _____

   _____

   _____

   _____

   _____

3. If you've answered the questions you should be able, with a bit of clever detective work, to figure out what the striking signwriters had written. Write what you think they wrote and give your reasons.

   _____

   _____

   _____

   _____

© World Teachers Press® – www.worldteacherspress.com

The Man in Red Sneakers

Joshua Ballico sat grim-faced in the courtroom. His mood became even more gloomy when he heard the testimony of his former business partner, Jordan Greenwood.

"Mr. Greenwood," said Chief Prosecutor Christopher Fishlock, "you say that Mr. Ballico was short of cash and had outstanding bills?"

"Yes, I could see that the business was headed for trouble," answered Greenwood. "Joshua is a nice guy but he has no head for business. Last week we decided to call it quits. We sold yesterday— fifty thousand in cash, we got."

"And what became of that fifty thousand dollars?" asked Fishlock.

"Well, the new owners gave us a week to get ourselves organized and move out of the building. I left the money they paid us in the safe overnight. In the morning, I sent young Dayne MacDougal, our clerk, to the bank with it. It would have been his last official job for the business. What a way to finish up! As you know, he was found unconscious in Wishbone Alley. The briefcase wide open—money gone!"

"And you say you saw the accused, Mr. Ballico, in his car at the crime scene. What makes you think he had something to do with the crime?" asked the chief prosecutor.

"I felt uncomfortable about sending young MacDougal with all that cash. I decided to catch up with him and drive him to the bank. As I turned into Wishbone Alley I saw Joshua sitting in his car. The motor was running. When he saw me he put his foot down and sped off. Then I saw Dayne, lying on the pavement, unconscious. I ran over to see him bleeding from a head wound. Thank goodness he's okay. Anyway, all that money was gone but his red sneaker was lying nearby," said Greenwood, pointing to Ballico.

"Can you be sure it was Mr. Ballico?" asked Fishlock.

"Sure I'm sure," said Greenwood. "I recognized the car and I saw him as he sped past. He must've lost the sneaker in the struggle because he was only wearing one red sneaker."

"Thank you. You may step down," said Chief Prosecutor Fishlock.

"Your witness," said the judge to Stephanie Sanderson, the bright young lawyer who was defending Ballico.

"Your Honor, my client is innocent. I'd like to call Mr. Greenwood back. His story is a lie and I will prove it so we can stop wasting the court's time and dismiss this case," she said confidently. 👁

How did defense lawyer Sanderson know that Greenwood's story was a lie?

1. Using different colors, draw lines to match the words to their meanings.

testimony •   • the person on trial for a crime

prosecutor •   • doing something with belief in oneself

accused •   • paved path for pedestrians on the side of a road

pavement •   • a statement made in a court of law

confidently •   • a public official who is in charge of the
                                 case against someone accused of a crime

Read all the evidence you have carefully.

2. Write short answers to the questions below.

(a) Who was accused of a crime in the story?

_____

(b) Who was the accused's business partner?

_____

(c) How much money did they get when they

sold the business?_____

(d) Where was the money left overnight?

_____

(e) Who was taking the money to the bank?

_____

(f) What happened to the money?

_____

(g) Who did Greenwood see at the crime scene?

_____

(h) Where was Ballico sitting when Greenwood saw him at the crime scene?

_____

(i) What did Ballico do when he saw Greenwood?

_____

(j) What clue was left near the unconscious

MacDougal? _____

(k) Why did Greenwood say the missing sneaker must have belonged to Ballico?

_____

(l) Where was Ballico sitting when Greenwood saw that he was only wearing one sneaker?

_____

3. Can you work out why the lawyer, Stephanie Sanderson, was so confident that Jordan Greenwood was telling lies?

_____

_____

The Guilty Gambler

"Come quickly! I've just been robbed!" panted Scott Spencer to the desk clerk at Centerville Police Station.

"It all happened so quickly … had to run all the way here 'cause I didn't have enough money for the taxi fare. There's a taxi stand out the front of my apartment."

"Okay! Slow down! Take it easy!" said the police officer who entered moments after Spencer. "I'm Officer Nicholas Cook. Get in the car and I'll drive you back to your place."

The young police officer ushered Spencer into the police patrol car. "Now, take a deep breath, slow down, and tell me what happened."

"It happened just now," said Spencer. "I'd just woken up … went to the casino last night. Won a lot, too! Oh boy, you should have seen me!"

"Okay, just tell me what happened this morning," said Officer Cook.

"Well, as I said, I'd just woken up. I heard a knock and opened the front door. Next thing I'm grabbed by two men. One of them held me down while the other went through all my drawers and ransacked the place. I had some of my girlfriend Eleanor's jewelry in a drawer…expensive stuff…over

ten thousand dollars worth. All gone! Ooooh, she'll be mad at me! Luckily I'd hidden the money I won at the casino under my bed. They didn't get that. Anyway, they ran off and I ran straight to the police station. Uh, just stop here, officer, my apartment's in this building."

Spencer showed the policeman into his apartment. It was a mess, with household items and clothing strewn everywhere.

"See the mess they made?" said Spencer.

Peter's Pawnbrokers
Instant cash for your unwanted items.
13 Bludge Rd, Downinowt

"Yes, and once you've cleaned up this mess there's another one you need to clean up back at the station," said the young policeman. "I think you might've sold your girlfriend's jewelry to pay some gambling debts. Your story doesn't add up." 👁

Why do you think Officer Cook was suspicious of Spencer's story? Gather all the evidence by answering the questions on the next page. They should help you see that Spencer wasn't being entirely truthful.

Check out the facts!

1. Using different colors, draw lines to match the words with their meanings.

patrol car •   • showed or guided someone

panted •   • building where gambling games are played

ushered •   • breathed with short, quick breaths

ransacked •   • a car driven by a policeman on duty

casino •   • hurriedly went through a place, stealing things and causing damage

2. Write short answers to the questions below.

(a) Who claimed he had just been robbed?

_____

(b) How did Spencer get to the police station?

_____

(c) Why hadn't he caught a taxi?

_____

(d) What was out in front of his apartment?

_____

(e) Who drove Spencer back to his apartment?

_____

(f) Where did Spencer say he'd been the previous

night? _____

(g) What did Spencer mean when he said, "Won a lot, too!"?

_____

_____

(h) How many men grabbed Spencer when he answered the knock at the door?

_____

(i) What did he say they had stolen?

_____

(j) Why didn't the robbers find the money Spencer said he had won at the casino?

_____

_____

3. If you have studied the evidence, you will probably have decided that, like many gamblers, Scott Spencer is a dishonest boaster. He had been to the casino that night but certainly hadn't won anything. He had, as Officer Cook said, gone to the casino to settle some outstanding debts from earlier losses. His need to be seen as a "winner" caused him to wind up a big-time loser in prison.

Tell how Officer Cook knew Spencer's plan for the big "fix up" had become a big "mix up."

_____

_____

Snow Job

The Hindmarsh brothers were the terrors of the small winter holiday town of Bear Lake.

Things often went missing when the two of them were around. Their favorite victims were unsuspecting people on vacations who rented cabins in Bear Lake to escape the city rat race for a while. The brothers lived in a shack right next to the cabins.

"What a lovely quiet place, Mavis," said Detective Mitchell Bagwill to his wife.

"Well, if there's one thing you need, my darling, it's peace and quiet, and you're going to have two weeks of it," replied Mavis.

"Yes, you're right. Two weeks here and I should be plenty rested," said the Detective as he kissed his wife goodnight.

A light, steady snowfall through the night gave Bear Lake a beautiful white carpet by the next morning.

The first people to wake in Bear Lake that morning were the Hindmarsh brothers. Before first light, they were hard at work. With the deserted streets of Bear Lake to themselves, they decided to go to work with their tools of trade, a flashlight and a brick.

Shining the flashlight through the window of Detective Bagwill's car, they saw something interesting on the front seat—Mavis Bagwill's expensive video camera. Shattering the side window with the brick, they grabbed the camera and quickly scooted back to their shack.

Fifteen minutes later, the first feeble rays of daylight peeped over the horizon. Mavis Bagwill was the third person in Bear Lake to open her eyes that morning. Looking outside she was pleased to see a deer's footprints leading up to the cabin door. The streets were still deserted, beautifully covered by the previous night's snowfall. Her delight, however, soon turned to alarm when she looked a little further. She saw the smashed side window of the car.

"Mitch! Wake up!" she exclaimed. "Someone's broken into the car!"

Detective Bagwill dressed quickly and went to the crime scene. He looked for a short time and then started in the direction of the Hindmarsh brothers' shack.

"Where are you going?" asked Mavis.

"I'm going over to that shack about 50 yards away. Whoever lives there stole our camera," said the Detective.

Within an hour the Hindmarsh brothers were in Bear Lake's lockup.

"Say, cop," said Glen, the younger of the two, "how'd you know it was us? Tell us. We have to know."

Detective Bagwill said nothing. He headed back to his cabin to resume a well-deserved vacation.

Use your comprehension and detective skills to find out how Detective Bagwill knew that the brothers were the culprits.

1. Write short answers to the questions below.

   (a) Why did people usually choose Bear Lake

   for a vacation? _____

   _____

   (b) Who was vacationing there with his wife? _____

   (c) What was the weather like during the night? _____

   (d) What did the snow look like? _____

   (e) Who were the first people to wake the next morning? _____

   (f) What were their tools of trade? _____

   (g) What was on the front seat of the Bagwills' car? _____

   (h) Where did the brothers go after stealing the camera? _____

   (i) Who was the third person awake that morning? _____

   (j) What did the streets look like? _____

   _____

   (k) What alarmed Mavis? _____

   (l) How far was the Hindmarsh brothers' shack from the Bagwill's cabin? _____

2. With the clues at your disposal, and using some clever detective thinking, you will be able to figure out how the Detective so easily directed his attentions to the shack of the Hindmarsh brothers.

   _____

   _____

   _____

   _____

   _____

3. List the names of America's five Great Lakes. You can find them in an atlas or on the Internet.

   _____

   _____

   _____

   _____

   _____

The Big Burger Bungle

The painters had been busy at Holly Town Shopping Mall. The interiors had been done and the mall looked very neat.

World of Grease
Holly Town

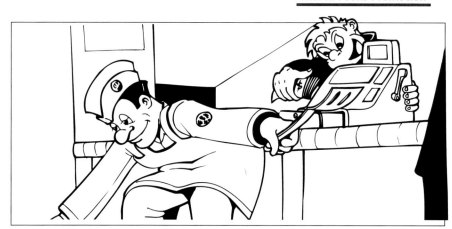

Health Foods Promotion

"Okay, boss. We've just done all the bench seats. Wow! Eleven o' clock! Looks like we get off early today," said painter John Gilmore. Bruce Bailey, chief cook and bottle washer at the World of Grease Burger Bar in the mall, wasn't so happy.

At the same time as Gilmore was celebrating his early finish for the day, Bailey had put through a call to mall management.

"Mr. Sparrow, it's me, from World of Grease. I've just been robbed. I was just bending over to pick up an onion ring I'd dropped on the floor. As I looked up to put it back on the hotplate, I saw a young fellow I'd just served rifling through my cash register. He stuffed all the cash I had into his pockets and ran off. The worst part of all was he didn't even pay for his burger. I'd recognize him if I saw him again, though. He hangs around the mall quite a bit."

"Better get the police involved, Bruce," said Mr. Sparrow.

When the police arrived, they suggested looking at some surveillance tapes taken by the mall's video cameras. While they did not show footage of the actual robbery, Bruce did recognize the culprit on the shot that showed people entering the mall's main doors.

"That's him, the one in the pink track pants and running shoes," he exclaimed.

"It's young Phil Benton," said Sergeant Gordon Milton. "We know him well. Come with us, Mr. Bailey, and we'll see what he's got to say."

Benton greeted his visitors with a smug grin. He was still wearing his clean, new, pink track pants.

"You say you've got me on tape. Well, you probably have. I did go to the mall this morning. And yes, I did buy a Greaseburger. But I know that won't show on the tape. The cameras don't cover World of Grease. A pity because then they'd prove my innocence."

"Anyway, I sat down on the benches near World of Grease and ate the burger.

"After that I headed off home . . . just got here a minute or so before you."

"It's him! He's the one!" shrieked Bailey. Such was his fury that foam was appearing in the corners of his mouth.

Restraining him, Sergeant Milton said calmly, "Don't worry Mr. Bailey. I know Benton's story isn't true. He'll have to get used to prison food for a while."

Use your comprehension and detective skills to find out how Sergeant Milton knew that Benton was lying.

1. Write short answers to the questions below.

   (a) Which workers had been busy at Holly Town Shopping Mall? _____

   (b) At what time had they finished?   (c) What was the last thing they painted?

   _____   _____

   (d) Where did Bruce Bailey work? _____

   (e) What was his job? _____

   (f) Who was the shopping mall manager? _____

   (g) Why had Bailey been bending over? _____

   (h) What did he see happening? _____
   (i) What did the police want to look at?   (j) What was Benton wearing?

   _____   _____

   (k) Why wouldn't the surveillance tape show Benton stealing from the cash register?

   _____

   (l) Why did Benton say it was a pity that the tape didn't show him at the World of Grease?

   _____

   (m) Where did Benton say he ate the burger? _____

   (n) What did Sergeant Milton say Benton would have to get used to? _____

2. On a sheet of paper, make 10 words of at least 3 letters using the letters in HAMBURGER. You may only use each letter the number of times it occurs (i.e. "R" can be used twice in a word like "RARE"— all other letters can only be used once in a word).

3. Sergeant Milton quickly decided that Benton was lying. You should be able to as well.

   _____
   _____
   _____
   _____

Farmer McSwine

We like to think that most people have a good side to them.

Farmer McSwine was not like most people. He'd been nasty since he was a baby. Now, at the age of sixty, he was as nasty as ever. In fact, he was nastier than ever. He'd had sixty years of practice.

The worst part of all was that he was clever. If he was called to account for his dreadful deeds, he always seemed to come up with a believable excuse for what happened. This time, though, he'd gone too far.

Poor little Bo Wilson had been shot in the leg with a pellet gun while walking past McSwine's farm. He'd limped to McSwine's fence and fallen through it. Police Officer Jazmin Sinadinos, part of the search party when Bo's mother raised the alarm that he was missing, found him sitting in McSwine's yard.

"I'll admit I went too far shooting at the boy, but you'll have to be a bit lenient with me," said McSwine.

"Oh? Why so?" asked Officer Sinadinos.

"Well…as you know, I raise roosters on this farm. Sell 'em to farmers around the district who want to increase their stocks. Well, I've seen this little beggar on my farm more than a dozen times—warned him off every time but he just keeps coming back. I even called his mother and warned her that if she didn't do something then I would. He's lately taken to stealing the eggs. Sells 'em to stores around here. What am I supposed to do? If I call the police, they give me the usual story—they're too busy to attend to such a small matter…they're understaffed and so on. Okay, I took a shot at him with that toy gun, but can't you understand how I felt? He was slowly bleeding me dry. Those birds and those eggs are my livelihood."

"No, I can't understand how you felt and I hope I never do. It must be awful to be like you," replied Officer Sinadinos. "The story you just told me is one big lie. I hope that the judge throws the book at you." 👁

You, the comprehension detective, must find out how Officer Sinadinos knew Farmer McSwine was not telling the truth.

1. Find the dictionary meaning of "misdemeanor." _____

_____

2. Write short answers to the questions below.

(a) For how many years had Farmer McSwine been nasty? _____

(b) What had McSwine done to Bo Wilson? _____

(c) What had he used? _____

(d) What did McSwine raise on his farm? _____

(e) How often had Farmer McSwine seen young Bo on his farm? _____

(f) What did McSwine say Bo had been stealing? _____

(g) What did he say Bo did with the items he stole? _____

(h) What did McSwine say the police did if he called and told them about the thefts?

_____

3. Because you have read the story and answered the questions thoughtfully, you should be able to tell why Officer Sinadinos knew McSwine was lying. Tell how he slipped up.

_____

_____

4. Match these "bird proverb" beginnings and endings.

A bird in the hand	•	• that lays the golden eggs.
Birds of a feather	•	• before they hatch.
Don't count your chickens	•	• is good for the gander.
Don't kill the goose	•	• catches the worm.
One swallow	•	• is worth two in the bush.
The early bird	•	• flock together.
What's good for the goose	•	• does not make summer.

Good Morning, Sunshine

It was a pleasant, sunny morning in Los Angeles.

The weather, however, did not match the early morning mood in Kelly's Jewelry shop.

"Help! Police! We've been robbed!" pleaded the distraught Sara Warrender.

Sara had only been working in the shop for a week. She'd come to work early at 6:00 a.m. to help the store manager change some price tags and arrange the window display.

"Tell us what happened," said Ryan Mate, the smart young police officer who was sent to attend to the robbery.

"Well," said the pretty young shop assistant, "I was putting out the display in the front window of the shop. Miss Aspey, that's my boss, just slipped out for a minute to grab a cup of coffee—neither of us has had any breakfast. Anyway, as I bent down to put a display tray in the window I sensed someone else was in the shop. I heard Miss Aspey scream as she was returning from the coffee shop. I turned around and saw a man running from the shop with a handful of expensive watches. He jumped into a car—he'd left the motor running. It was white and had a surfboard on top. I'm not sure what model it was. I don't know much about cars. Oh yes, it had Florida number plates."

Officer Mate radioed this information to all patrol cars. Inside ten minutes the vigilant officers of the police department had pulled over a white car with Florida number plates and with a surfboard on top. The driver, a young surfer who called himself "Tiny" Hicks, seemed rather agitated.

"You've got the wrong guy," he protested. "I'm over here on a surfing vacation—only got to L.A. yesterday.

Slept on the beach. Yeah, I was up early all right but I was nowhere near the shopping center where this jewelry shop is."

"I love watching the sun rise up out of the ocean. I do it all the time back home in Miami. Wow! It was something else this morning … that big sun rising up out of the Pacific Ocean! Something else! Real cool, man! Hey, it was cooler than cool! Like…"

"Yeah, real cool," said Renato Puda, the young police officer who'd pulled the car over. "If you like things cool, you'll be enjoying some time in our cooler. I think that could be where you're going. Do you want to have another try at your story? I don't think you were at the beach this morning. I think you were at Kelly's Jewelry shop, helping yourself to some unearned money." 👁

Use your own detective skills to find out why the police officer was suspicious of Hick's story.

1. Write short answers to the question below.

    (a) In which city is the story set? _____

    (b) At what time had Sara Warrender started work that morning? _____

    (c) What was she doing when the robbery took place? _____

    _____

    (d) Why had Miss Aspey left the shop? _____

    (e) What had the thief stolen? _____

    (f) List three things Sara mentioned when describing the car. _____

    _____

    (g) Who was the driver of the car that was pulled over? _____

    (h) Why did Hicks say he was visiting Los Angeles? _____

    (i) Where did Hicks say he spent the previous night? _____

    (j) What did he say he loved to watch? _____

    (k) Which ocean did he say the sun rose over? _____

3. Answer NORTH, SOUTH, EAST, or WEST to the questions below.

    (a) From which direction does the sun rise? _____

    (b) In which direction does the sun set?

    _____

    (c) In which direction would you travel if going from Los Angeles to San Diego?

    _____

    (d) If traveling from Colorado to Montana, in which direction would you be going?

    _____

4. How did Police Officer Puda know that Hicks's story was a lie?

    _____

    _____

    _____

    _____

    _____

    _____

    _____

The Botched Birthday Theft

"Yes, Miss Wilcox, we're looking into it," said the postal security investigator, Amy Fealy.

She was talking to young Emily Wilcox who had sent her mother an expensive watch as a birthday present. Miss Wilcox's mother had not received it. There was no record of it leaving the mail center. Suspicion fell upon three postal workers who worked in the special parcels and packages department.

"Follow me, Miss Wilcox. I'm going to question three people who may be able to help us retrieve your mother's present," said Amy.

Miss Wilcox followed her down a flight of stairs and along a wide corridor. The special investigator asked to speak to the three workers separately.

To each in turn she said, "I'm going to ask you a number of questions about a package which was sent from here on December 9, containing an expensive gift for Miss Wilcox's mother. It has disappeared and we believe it may have been stolen."

"You say it was on December 9. I was away on sick leave on December 8, 9, and 10," said Madison Cosgrove.

"I don't remember Miss Wilcox's package. As you know, we have hundreds of packages go through here every day," said Ruth O'Rafferty. "Anyway, I already have a watch. This one!" she went on, pointing to the expensive looking watch on her wrist. "Everyone who works here will tell you that it was presented to me by the boss last year to recognize my thirtieth year in the job. See, it's even got an inscription on the back: 'To Ruth for your many years of honest service'."

The third worker, Laura Graham, could not look Amy in the eye.

"I was at work that day, but I don't recall anything unusual. Only last week though, my purse disappeared with my month's pay check in it."

"Must've left you short of cash," said Amy.

"Yes. Luckily my brother lent me some money, otherwise I'd be unable to pay the rent or buy anything to eat. Do you know what it feels like when you've got six hungry kids at home and a husband who's lost his job?" replied Mrs Graham.

Amy thanked the workers and took Miss Wilcox aside.

"Don't worry, Miss Wilcox. Thieves usually think they're clever, but they're not. I know who took your package and she won't be working here much longer." 👁

Like Security Investigator Amy Fealy, you must examine the evidence. Perhaps then you'll be able to identify the rat in the postal workers' ranks.

Post

Send your mail anywhere. It's safe with us!

1. Write short answers to the questions below.

   (a) What was Amy Fealy's job?

   _____

   (b) What birthday present had Emily Wilcox sent her mother?

   _____

   (c) From which department were the three postal workers?

   _____

   (d) On which day had Emily mailed the package?

   _____

   (e) What did Emily tell the three workers the package contained? _____

   _____

   (f) When was Madison Cosgrove away on

   sick leave? _____

   (g) Why did Ruth O'Rafferty say it would be hard to remember Miss Wilcox's present?

   _____

   _____

   (h) What did Ruth O'Rafferty say she already have?

   _____

   (i) Why had she been given this watch?

   _____

   _____

   (j) What did Laura say had happened to her the

   week before? _____

   _____

2. A "motive" is a reason for doing something. Often it can be hidden or not obvious. One of the three workers has a clear motive to steal the expensive present. Who has a motive and what is the motive? Answer ... (person's name) because ... (their motive).

   _____ because _____.

3. Who appeared to be the most honest worker and why? Answer ... (name) because ... (motive).

   _____ because _____.

4. Good detectives always look beyond the obvious when trying to track down criminals. Carefully read the evidence you have gathered and tell who the guilty person was.

   _____

   _____

© World Teachers Press® – www.worldteacherspress.com

The Great Diamond Grab

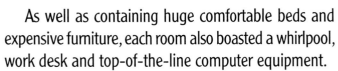

"And over there is a portrait of Sir Anthony Van Loon, who, in 1748, had this mansion built," said the tour guide.

She was talking to students from the elite Yarvard school.

As part of their studies in art, the students were touring the wealthy mansions of the United States.

After a formal, sit-down dinner, the young gentlemen made their way to their well-appointed rooms to rest and relax before continuing their tour on the following day.

As well as containing huge comfortable beds and expensive furniture, each room also boasted a whirlpool, work desk and top-of-the-line computer equipment.

Just as everyone was settling down at about nine o'clock that evening, the lights of the Van Loon mansion went out. Power was restored an hour later and a message came over the intercom asking all students to assemble in the huge dining room.

When everyone was gathered, they were told some dreadful news.

During the blackout, the fabulous Van Loon diamond had been stolen. This prized gem was valued at over a million dollars.

When asked to account for their movements, all the students except Kiefer Brown were able to verify their whereabouts during the time of the blackout.

"Okay," said Brown, "no one was with me during the blackout, but what does that prove? I wanted to be alone. I didn't even realize there was a blackout until now. I had an assignment on ethics to get finished. After dinner I went to my room, closed the door so as not to be disturbed, switched on the computer and went to work. I worked on right through the blackout—only just finished now," said Brown, his lip curling into an unconvincing grin.

"Do you stand by your story, Kiefer?" asked Mr. Gravelbart, the schoolmaster in charge of the touring group.

"Of course! I'm no liar!" said Brown.

"I'm afraid I'll have to call the police and let them talk to you about it then," continued Mr. Gravelbart. "I suggest you tell them the truth, however, not the lies you told all of us just now."

How did Mr. Gravelbart know that Brown's story was a lie?

1. Using different colors, draw lines to match the words with their meanings.

mansion •   • a group of people considered to be the best in a group or society

elite •   • the study of what is right and what is wrong

intercom •   • a two-way radio or communication device

verify •   • a large impressive house

ethics •   • to demonstrate that something is true

2. Write short answers to these questions.

(a) Which place were the students touring?

_____

(b) Where did the students go after dinner?

_____

(c) List four things that the rooms contained.

_____

_____

_____

_____

(d) What happened at nine o'clock in the

evening? _____

(e) For how long was the Van Loon mansion

without power? _____

(f) What was stolen during the blackout?

_____

(g) Who was unable to verify his whereabouts?

_____

(h) What did Brown say he'd been doing during

the blackout? _____

_____

(i) Who is Mr. Gravelbart? _____

_____

(j) Who did Mr. Gravelbart say he'd have to call
after hearing Brown's story?

_____

3. Are you as good a detective as Klaus Gravelbart, the teacher in this story? Explain why Brown's
story does not make sense.

_____

_____

The Breakfast Break-in

"I'll lose my job for sure," moaned the young man in the business suit. "What a way to start a Monday morning!"

His name was Alan Longmire, a slick salesman who worked at Hammo's Used Cars.

"Settle down, Mr. Longmire. We'll get to the bottom of this," said Officer Ebony Robinson.

"Just drink this cup of tea and tell us when you're ready," said her partner, Officer Sam Stubbs.

"Ahh! That's good!" said the young salesman. "Well, it all happened so quickly I don't know where to start. I'd just finished getting ready for work. I had my usual scrambled eggs and toast for breakfast. After cleaning up I was just relaxing a little—reading the paper. Next thing, without any warning, three men pushed my front door in. They ripped the locks clean off! Two of them held me down while the other one went to my safe. He must've been experienced at safecracking—only took him about a minute to open it. Whoosh! Sixty thousand dollars gone, just like that!"

"You said sixty thousand dollars?" gasped Officer Robinson. "Do you usually keep that much at home?"

"No! Never! We had a terrific day on Friday—sold a record number of cars. I worked late. The bank was closed so I called the boss and told him I'd look after the money for the weekend," replied Longmire.

"And you say this break-in happened half an hour ago?" said Officer Stubbs.

"Yes! After they left, I got into my car and drove straight here."

"You show us the way," said Officer Robinson. "We'll follow in the police car."

After a short drive, Longmire pulled into his driveway. He unlocked the front door of his expensive looking house and signalled to the police officers to follow him inside.

"What do you think of his story?" the officer asked her partner.

"It's got to be a lie. I know this fellow. They call him "Big Al" - a mad gambler. I'd say his boss's money was lost on the racetrack or at the casino on the weekend. The rest is a cover up."

"What do you suggest we do?" asked Officer Robinson with a smile.

"Arrest him," said Officer Stubbs.

The best dealer around for service and great prices **Hammo's** Used Cars

You must now look at all the information. When you have done this you will find why Officer Robinson does not believe Longmire's story.

1. Write short answers to the questions below.

(a) On which day of the week does the story take place?

_____

(b) Where did Alan Longmire work?

_____

(c) Which two police officers handled the case?

_____

_____

(d) What was Longmire doing just before the crime took place?

_____

(e) What did the three men do to gain entry into Longmire's house?

_____

(f) What happened to the door locks?

_____

(g) Why did Longmire think that the man who opened the safe was an experienced safecracker?

_____

(h) How much money was stolen?

_____

(i) Why wasn't the money taken to the bank?

_____

(j) How long, before Longmire contacted the police, had the break-in taken place?

_____

(k) How did Longmire enter his house when he brought the police officers back?

_____

(l) What was Longmire's nickname?

_____

(m) What did Officer Robinson think had really happened to the money?

_____

Book him, Daniel!

2. You have gathered a lot of vital information. Officer Stubbs took particular notice of some of the answers before Longmire was arrested. What was wrong with Longmire's story?

_____

_____

Who Got the Job?

The University of Sydney was in deep shock. The renowned entomologist, Sir Oscar Thorax, had passed away suddenly.

An entomologist studies insects and Sir Oscar should have known better. He'd been studying a new specimen from the tropics, carelessly left the lid off its jar and been bitten. Death was almost instantaneous. The offending insect was caught again but the world had lost one of its foremost authorities on insects and his students were to take the vital final exams in three months. A replacement had to be found quickly.

An advertisement was placed in all the major daily newspapers and on the Internet. After two weeks, interviews were arranged for the four final applicants. The chancellor of the university met them casually at dinner before their final interviews.

"How long have you been interested in the study of insects?" he asked John MacMillan, the first of the applicants.

"Oh, ever since I can remember," said MacMillan. "As a boy I used to collect them and study them. Beetles, butterflies and spiders were my favorite insects. I have extensive collections of these insects in my study at home."

Memorial Service for Sir Oscar Thorax
Insectopia Chapel, Bug Lane
Friday 17   10:00 a.m.
No flowers please.
All money to "Ban Insecticide" campaign

"I see," said the Chancellor. "And you, Miss Judd. Tell me something about your background in the field," he said, turning to the another applicant, Mary Judd.

"Well, I was always afraid of them. As a child I remember looking into the mirror and seeing the four hairy legs of a bull ant crawling up my collar. I flicked it off, put it in a bottle and was hooked on insects from then on."

"That must have been very frightening for you," said the Chancellor politely.

"My background is in polar exploration," volunteered Kevin Boston, another applicant for the position. "Last winter at the South Pole, I did a detailed study of the insect life I found there at the time. There were some beautiful butterfly specimens," he said.

The last applicant, Godwin Austen, told of how he had worked at several other universities over a period of thirty years.

When the dinner was over and the guests had gone, the Chancellor confided to his wife, "It's going to be a lot easier to choose Professor Thorax's replacement than I thought it would be. In fact, I'm only going to interview one of the applicants". 👁

With a bit of elementary scientific research and a study of your answers to the questions, you, the Comprehension Detective, should be able to discover who got the interview.

1. Write short answers to the questions below.

(a) What is an entomologist? _____

(b) What had Sir Oscar done to cause his untimely death? _____

_____

(c) Where was the job advertised? _____

(d) How many final applicants were there for the job? _____

(e) What did John MacMillan say were his favorite insects? _____

_____

(f) Which insect did Mary Judd claim made her interested in entomology? _____

(g) Where did Kevin Boston say he'd studied insects? _____

(h) In which season did he say he did this study? _____

(i) What was Godwin Austen's background? _____

(j) How many body parts do insects have? _____ (k) How many legs? _____

(l) Who do you think got the job? _____

2. Write sentences when doing the exercise below.

Three people were unsuccessful in their bid for the job because they quite clearly did not have even a basic knowledge of insects. In each case, this was the vital flaw that let the Chancellor know that they were not qualified for the job. Tell why each of them missed out.

- _____

_____

- _____

_____

- _____

_____

Save the Panther!

It had been one of the hottest summers on record in New York City, but the banner headline on the cover of the New York Times helped some people breathe a little easier.

"Panther Caught!" it read on that July fourth. The headline referred to a jewel thief who had plundered millions from wealthy jewelry owners across the country.

He was called "The Panther" because he was always dressed in black, was as silent as one of these big cats stalking its prey, and disappeared into the night's blackness when his work was done. No one had ever seen his face.

As often happens, police stumbled onto their suspect while seeking smaller game. In a routine check of hotel suites looking for an offender who hadn't paid his parking fines, they came into the Panther's rooms by accident. One sharp-eyed officer noted a diamond necklace which had been carelessly left on the floor under a newspaper. Further investigation found his drawers stuffed with jewelry worth a fortune. The suspect, a smooth-talking pretty boy named James Flett, was an Australian.

"But I only arrived in the country a week ago!" pleaded Flett. "This Panther fellow has been operating for over a year according to your papers. Check at the hotel. You'll see! I only booked into this hotel a week ago, just after I landed in this country. Why, just over a week ago I was in my home town, Melbourne, sunning myself on St. Kilda Beach. There must be at least a hundred people there who saw me and could identify me. The place was packed sardine-tight!"

A check with the booking clerk at the hotel confirmed Flett's story. He had only booked into the hotel that week.

The officers spoke between themselves, considering what they should do next. "This guy says he's from Australia. Where's that?" asked the first.

"Get a map of the world and look near the bottom," said his more senior partner.

"Maybe we should call the police down there to check this guy's story. Maybe he was sunning himself on a beach down there a week ago, like he says."

"I doubt it very much," said the senior officer. "We've got our man all right. He's not only a thief, he's a liar too." 👁

You, the Comprehension Detective, must find out why the senior officer didn't believe Flett's story.

1. Find the dictionary meaning of "alibi." _____

_____

2. Write short answers to the questions below.

(a) What was the date when the headline

appeared? _____

(b) Which season was it?

_____

(c) Which newspaper was mentioned?

_____

(d) What name was coined for the jewel thief?

_____

(e) List two ways in which the thief was like a

panther. _____

_____

(f) What did the sharp-eyed officer see?

_____

(g) From which country was Flett?

_____

(h) How long did Flett say he'd been in the U.S.?

_____

(i) Where did he say he'd been immediately

before this? _____

(j) What did he say he'd been doing there?

_____

(k) When had he booked into the hotel?

_____

(l) In which hemisphere is the U.S.?

| northern | southern |

(m) In which hemisphere is Australia?

| northern | southern |

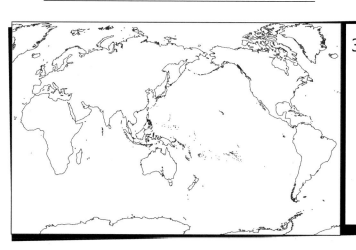

3. On the world map, color Australia red, North America green, South America orange, Europe purple, Africa yellow, and Asia blue. Label New York City and Melbourne.

4. Your sharp detective's brain should tell you why the senior officer knew that Flett was lying.

_____

_____

Mental Muscle Flexing .... Page 7
radio

Follow the Clues .... Page 8
1. 17 muffins　　　　　2. 18 runs
3. 45 marbles　　　　　4. 1 goal

The Case of the Pilfered Purse .... Page 9–10
1. (a) Detective Avila, Sarah Sontner, Elmer, Butch, Adrian Corney
   (b) Sarah Sontner's purse　(c) poodle - Maltese cross
   (d) barked and growled at them　(e) ID, cards, $5000 cash
   (f) one day　(g) her boyfriend, Adrian Corney
   (h) Elmer the mailman　(i) dozing, sleeping
   (j) how the intruder had escaped harm at the spiteful jaws of Butch
   (k) Walked across to him quietly wagging his tail
2. Miss Sontner had only been in New York for one day, not long enough to befriend anyone. Butch barked and growled at strangers but did not behave like this when he knew someone well. There was no sign of Butch having attacked an intruder and there had been no barking to wake Sarah up. It is likely, Detective Avila reasoned, that the intruder was known by Butch and that he did not create a fuss, just as he didn't when Adrian entered the apartment.
3. A book that lists words in groups of synonyms.
4. Teacher Check.

Eliminating Suspects .... Page 11
1. Stanley　　　　　2. (a)

Grubby Gregory .... Pages 12–13
1. (a) messy　(b) left them on the floor
   (c) baseball bat, football, toy　(d) put anything back in its place
   (e) she could clean her house　(f) exhausted
   (g) go straight to bed　(h) brush his teeth
   (i) ironing　(j) under the sink
   (k) in the rack　(l) in the rack
   (m) her house was tidy　(n) brush his teeth
2. Gregory never put anything back in its place yet his toothbrush was in the rack and the toothpaste was in its place under the sink.

The Fast-footed Felon .... Pages 14–15
1. (a) lazy, untrustworthy　(b) quite clever, a good runner
   (c) too lazy to cope with the hard training
   (d) snatching wallets, purses, etc. (e) motorcycle
   (f) to register the motorcycle　(g) turned the handle; pushed
   (h) keys and a wallet　(i) turned the handle and pushed
   (j) before he left the motor registry
2. (a) bee　(b) nails
   (c) bat　(d) mouse
   (e hills　(f) daisy
3. Denver pushed open the door when entering the motor registry. When he tried to leave he also pushed it. He should have pulled.

Colin, the Coin Con Man .... Pages 16–17
1. (a) coins　(b) more than a year
   (c) over $200　(d) to buy some coins for his collection
   (e) Mr. Colin Ryan　(f) American coins
   (g) old American dollars　(h) small; dull-colored
   (i) Ancient Rome　(j) Julius Caesar
   (k) 55 B.C.　(l) a crook
2. obverse – the side of a coin showing the head or main design
   reverse – the side of a coin bearing the value and secondary design
3. B.C. – before Christ
   A.D. – Anno Domini (indicates the number of years after Christ's birth)
4. Coins were never dated "B.C." How could they be? That would mean they knew in advance that Jesus was to be born on a particular date. The first European coins with dates on them appeared in the mid 16th century (1550s), 1,500 years after Julius Caesar's time.

Fresh Fruit-O for Sale-O! .... Pages 18–19
1. (a) Mr. George, Samantha O'Brian, Evan Gussey
   (b) Mr. George　(c) stealing strawberries from his shop
   (d) a lunchbox　(e) his Uncle Paul's farm
   (f) his uncle's strawberry tree
2.
3. low growing plant which produces soft red fruit with a seed-studded surface
4. Strawberries do not grow on trees.

The Big Strike .... Pages 20–21
1. (a) they felt they were underpaid　(b) they were paid handsome salaries
   (c) go on strike immediately　(d) to stop working
   (e) a big rally　(f) a protest sign
   (g) Man can not live on chalk alone.
   (h) dogcatcher　(i) paint signs
2. teacher check
3. The workers decided to go on strike immediately. To go on strike means to stop working. A signwriter's job entails painting signs. Since they were on strike, the signwriters could not do their jobs, so their placards had nothing at all painted on them.

The Man in Red Sneakers .... Pages 22–23
1.
   testimony — a statement made in a court of law
   prosecutor — a public official who is in charge of the case against someone accused of a crime
   accused — the person on trial for a crime
   pavement — paved path for pedestrians on the side of a road
   confidently — doing something with belief in oneself
2. (a) Joshua Ballico　(b) Jordon Greenwood
   (c) fifty thousand dollars　(d) in the safe
   (e) Dayne MacDougal　(f) it was stolen
   (g) Joshua Ballico　(h) in his car
   (i) sped away　(j) a red sneaker
   (k) he was only wearing one sneaker
   (l) in his car
3. Greenwood said he saw Ballico sitting in his car with only one sneaker on. If he was sitting in his car it would not be possible for Greenwood to see what Ballico was wearing on his feet.

The Guilty Gambler .... Pages 24–25
1.
   patrol car — a car driven by a policeman on duty
   panted — breathed with short, quick breaths
   ushered — showed or guided someone
   ransacked — hurriedly went through a place, stealing things and causing damage.
   casino — building where gambling games are played
2. (a) Scott Spencer　(b) ran
   (c) didn't have enough money to pay a taxi fare
   (d) taxi stand　(e) Officer Cook
   (f) casino　(g) he had won a lot of money
   (h) two　(i) his girlfriend Eleanor's jewelry
   (j) hidden under his bed
3. He boasted that he had won a lot of money at the casino and yet he didn't have money to pay for a taxi fare to the police station.

Snow Job .... Pages 26-27

1. (a) to escape the city rat race (b) Detective Mitchell Bagwill
    (c) there was a light steady snow (d) a beautiful white carpet
    (e) the Hindmarsh brothers (f) flashlight; brick
    (g) Mavis Bagwill's expensive video camera
    (h) to their shack (i) Mavis Bagwill
    (j) deserted, beautifully covered with snow
    (k) seeing the smashed side window of the car
    (l) about fifty yards
2. It had snowed during the night and then stopped because the deer's footprints remained visible. Detective Inspector Bagwill just followed the footprints left by the Hindmarsh brothers from his car to their shack.
3. Superior, Michigan, Huron, Erie, Ontario

The Big Burger Bungle .... Pages 28–29

1. (a) painters (b) eleven o' clock
    (c) the bench seats (d) World of Grease Burger Bar
    (e) chief cook and bottlewasher (f) Mr Sparrow
    (g) to pick up an onion ring he had dropped
    (h) a young man rifling through his cash register
    (i) surveillance footage taken by the mall's video cameras
    (j) running shoes and pink track pants
    (k) cameras didn't cover World of Grease
    (l) it would have proved his innocence
    (m) on the benches near World of Grease
    (n) prison food
2. teacher check
3. Benton said he sat down on the benches near World of Grease. They had just been painted at the time of the robbery. Benton's track pants would have been marked by the paint.

Farmer McSwine .... Pages 30–31

1. misbehavior; misdeed; a less serious crime
2. (a) sixty (b) shot him in the leg
    (c) pellet gun (d) roosters
    (e) more than a dozen times (f) eggs
    (g) sold them to stores
    (h) said they were too busy, understaffed, etc.
3. McSwine said Bo was stealing eggs and selling them. He raised roosters, which do not lay eggs.
4.
A bird in the hand	that lays the golden egg
Birds of a feather	before they are hatched
Don't count your chickens	is good for the gander
Don't kill the goose	catches the worm
One swallow	is worth two in the bush
The early bird	flock together
What's good for the goose	does not make summer

Good Morning, Sunshine .... Pages 32–33

1. Teacher check
2. (a) Los Angeles (b) 6:00 a.m.
    (c) putting out the display in the shop's front window
    (d) to get a cup of coffee (e) a handful of expensive watches
    (f) white; surfboard on top; Florida number plates
    (g) "Tiny" Hicks (h) on a surfing holiday
    (i) on the beach (j) the sun rising over the ocean
    (k) the Pacific Ocean
3. (a) east (b) west
    (c) south (d) north
4. Hicks had probably slept on the beach and watched the sun rise over the ocean in Florida, which is on the eastern side of America. In Los Angeles, however, the sun rises over the vast mass of land of the North American continent, not over water.

The Botched Birthday Theft .... Pages 34–35

1. (a) postal security investigator (b) an expensive watch
    (c) parcels and packages (d) December 9
    (e) an expensive gift (f) December 8, 9, 10
    (g) hundreds of packages were handled there every day
    (h) a watch (i) for 30 years of honest service
    (j) her purse had disappeared
2. Laura Graham because her purse had been stolen, leaving her short of money
3. Ruth O'Rafferty because she had been acknowledged for service and honesty
4. Ruth O'Rafferty is the thief. Amy Fealy told each worker only that the stolen gift was valuable. O'Rafferty, however, knew that the stolen item was a watch.

The Great Diamond Grab .... Pages 36–37

1.
mansion	a group of people considered to be the best
elite	the study of what is right and what is wrong
intercom	a two-way radio or communication device
verify	a large impressive house
ethics	to demonstrate that something is true

2. (a) Van Loon mansion (b) to their rooms
    (c) beds, expensive furniture, whirlpool, workdesk, computer equipment
    (d) the lights went out/power cut (e) one hour
    (f) the Van Loon Diamond (g) Kiefer Brown
    (h) using the computer to do an assignment on ethics
    (i) schoolmaster in charge of the touring group
    (j) the police
3. Brown said that he was working on the computer doing his ethics assignment during the blackout. A computer needs electricity to work.

The Breakfast Break-in .... Pages 38–39

1. (a) Monday (b) Hammo's Used Cars
    (c) Ebony Robinson, Sam Stubbs (d) reading the paper
    (e) pushed in the front door (f) they were ripped off
    (g) it only took him a minute to open the safe
    (h) sixty thousand dollars (i) the bank was closed
    (j) half an hour (k) unlocked the front door
    (l) Big Al (m) gambled it away on the racetrack
2. Longmire said the locks had been ripped off his front door yet he unlocked the door to enter the house. As the crime had allegedly occurred only half an hour earlier, this would not be enough time for the doors to have been repaired.

Who Got the Job? .... Pages 40–41

1. (a) someone who studies insects
    (b) left the lid off the jar containing a poisonous insect
    (c) newspapers, Internet (d) four
    (e) beetles, butterflies, and spiders
    (f) a bull ant (g) South Pole
    (h) winter
    (i) had worked at several universities over the past 30 years
    (j) three (k) six
    (l) Godwin Austen
2. • John MacMillan – thought spiders were insects
    • Mary Judd – said bull ants have four legs
    • Kevin Boston – claimed he was studying insects during an Antarctic winter. There are no insects at the South Pole.

Save the Panther! .... Pages 42–43

1. evidence that one was elsewhere when a crime was committed
2. (a) July 4th (b) summer
    (c) New York Times (d) the Panther
    (e) dressed in black, moved quietly, quickly disappeared into the darkness
    (f) a diamond necklace (g) Australia
    (h) one week (i) Melbourne
    (j) sunning himself on St. Kilda Beach
    (k) a week earlier (l) northern
    (m) southern
3. Teacher check
4. July is summertime for countries in the northern hemisphere but winter in the southern hemisphere. Flett would have presented an odd image, sunbathing on St. Kilda Beach in the middle of winter, and the beach certainly would not be packed "sardine-tight."